Clay Jewelry

Make a fashion statement with unique jewelry that's easy to craft using Sculpey® quality clays. No one will believe you made these yourself!

LEISURE ARTS, INC. • Maumelle, Arkansas

Ikat Bangle Bracelet

SHOPPING LIST

- ☐ premo! Sculpey Accents® Clay (2 oz): 1 pkg ***each*** of Pearl, Peacock Pearl, Purple Pearl, and Sunset Pearl
- ☐ premo! Sculpey® Clay (2 oz): 1 pkg of Wasabi
- ☐ Sculpey® Clay Conditioning Machine
- ☐ Sculpey® Acrylic Roller
- ☐ Sculpey® Super Slicer
- ☐ Sculpey® Technique Design Blocks
- ☐ Round, bakeable object the same circumference as your desired bracelet (we used a cookie cutter)
- ☐ 20-gauge wire in 3 coordinating colors (optional)
- ☐ seed beads in coordinating colors (optional)
- ☐ Wire cutters (optional)
- ☐ Damp paper towels or baby wipes

To make the Basic Bracelet:

Please read the General Instructions on pages 22- 23 before beginning your project.

Measure your wrist/hand to determine the circumference the bracelet needs to be to slip on and off comfortably.

1. Using the #2 setting on the clay machine and working with one color at a time from lightest to darkest, condition each color of clay.

2. Mix about an 1/8 of a package each of Pearl and Wasabi to make Wasabi Pearl. Mix about an 1/8 of a package each of Pearl and Peacock Pearl to make Double Pearl Peacock.

3. Using the #1 setting on the clay machine, make an approximately 8" x 2" sheet of Pearl. Trim the sheet to 7" x 1 1/4". Make an approximately 3 1/2" x 2" sheet of each color, Wasabi Pearl, Double Pearl Peacock, Purple Pearl, and Sunset Pearl. Trim each sheet to 3" x 1 1/2" ***(Fig. 1)***.

Fig. 1

4. Cut approximately twelve 1/8" wide strips of each color ***(Fig. 2)***. **Note:** Thicker strips will produce wider bands of color and thinner strips will produce more stripes on the finished bracelet.

Fig. 2

Designed by Amy Koranek

5. Leaving about 1/8" or less of Pearl showing between colors, lay the strips across the Pearl rectangle. It is fine if the strips twist or are not spaced exactly the same distance apart ***(Fig. 3)***. **Note:** Leaving more space between strips will produce wider stripes of Pearl on the finished bracelet.

Fig. 3

6. Use the acrylic roller to secure the strips to the Pearl rectangle. This will also secure the rectangle to the work surface to keep it in place for Step 7.

7. To make the ikat design, always hold the Dragging Design Block at a 45° angle to the clay. Start at one end and drag the tool across the strips, creating shallow grooves in the clay and dragging one color into the next ***(Fig. 4)***. Use the acrylic roller to *slightly* flatten the grooves. Making sure the long edges are straight, trim the strips even with the sides of the rectangle.

Fig. 4

8. Using any color desired, roll a 1/2" x 8" log of clay. Keeping the beginning edge straight along the length of the log ***(Fig. 5)***, roll the rectangle around the log; trim the rectangle to fit.

Fig. 5

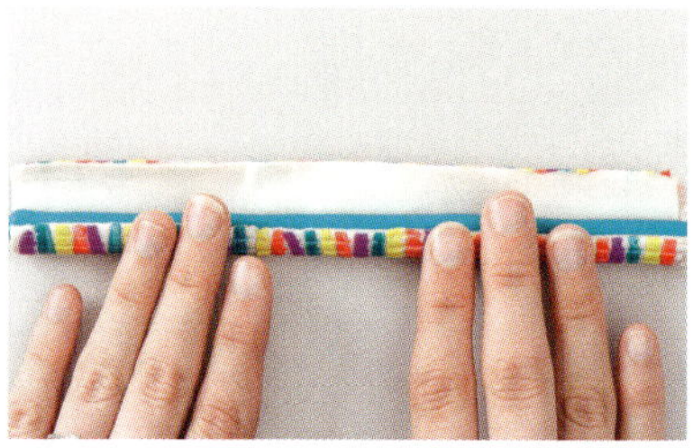

9. Roll and twist the log by hand. As you work, tiny lines will start to appear in the colors. Continue rolling and twisting until the log is about 3/8" in diameter and slightly longer than your determined bracelet size.

10. Trim the log with angled ends to the exact size needed to fit around your baking form. Wrap the log around the form and use your fingers to securely smooth the ends together. Follow the manufacturer's instructions to bake and cool.

To add the trims:

11. For the clay trimmed bracelet, twist and roll a leftover log piece to about an 1/8" dia. Cut four 2 1/2"-3 1/2" lengths and roll the ends to taper ***(Fig. 6)***. Spacing evenly, wrap the lengths around the bracelet and bake for 15 minutes; cool completely.

Fig. 6

12. For the wire trimmed bracelet, cut one 10"-12" wire length of each color. Slide 3 beads to the center of 1 wire length. Holding the beads on the bracelet, work from the center out to wrap each wire end around the bracelet. Spacing evenly, repeat with remaining 2 wire lengths.

Lentil Bead Earrings

SHOPPING LIST

- ☐ premo! Sculpey® Clay (2 oz): 1 pkg ***each*** of Peacock Pearl, Bright Green Pearl, and Translucent
- ☐ Sculpey® Clay Conditioning Machine
- ☐ Sculpey® Bead Making Kit
- ☐ Sculpey® Acrylic Roller
- ☐ 2 3mm crystal beads
- ☐ 2 silver ear wires
- ☐ 2 silver eye pins with decorative heads
- ☐ Round-nose pliers, wire cutters
- ☐ Damp paper towels or baby wipes

Designed by Phoebe Doehring

To make the Earrings:

Please read the General Instructions on pages 22- 23 before beginning your project.

1. Using the #2 setting on the clay machine and working with one color at a time lightest to darkest, condition each color of clay.

2. Roll one 1/4" x 3" log of each color ***(Fig. 1)***. Twist the colors together, candy cane style, and roll. Fold the log in half and roll ***(Fig. 2)***. Continue folding and rolling until the clay has a marbled look ***(Fig. 3)***.

Fig. 1

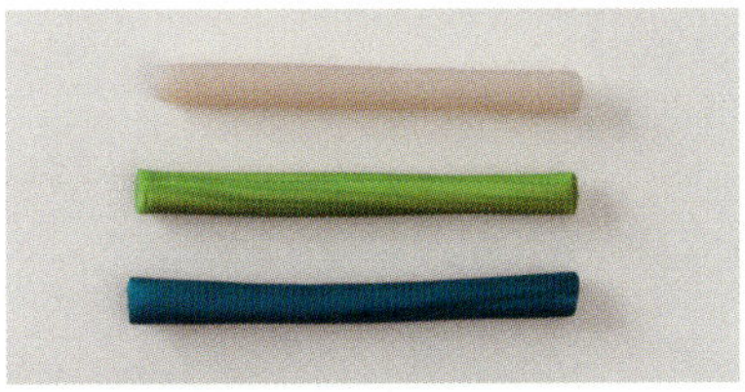

Fig. 2

Fig. 3

3. Cut 2 equal size pieces of clay 1/2" - 3/4" long from your log ***(Fig. 4)***. Roll each piece into a ball ***(Fig. 4)***.

Fig. 4

Instructions continued on page 7.

Opal Ring

SHOPPING LIST

- ☐ premo! Sculpy Accents® Clay (2 oz): 1 pkg ***each*** of Opal and Gold Glitter
- ☐ Sculpey® Clay Conditioning Machine
- ☐ Sculpey® 5-in-1 Tool Kit
- ☐ Sculpey® Super Slicer
- ☐ Sculpey® Acrylic Roller
- ☐ Metal ring finding
- ☐ Super glue
- ☐ Damp paper towels or baby wipes

Designed by Amy Koranek

To make the Ring:

Please read the General Instructions, pages 22- 23, before beginning your project.

1. Using the #1 setting on the clay machine and working with one color at a time, condition both colors of clay.

2. Roll an approximately 5/8" dia. ball of Opal ***(Fig. 1)***. To make the stone, shape the ball into a triangle with a rounded top and sides, and a flat bottom ***(Fig. 2)***.

Fig. 1

Fig. 2

3. Run the Gold Glitter through the clay machine on the #4 setting. Cut an approximately 1 1/2" square of Gold Glitter. Center and then press the stone into the square ***(Fig. 3)***. Trim the Gold Glitter even with the stone ***(Fig. 4)***.

Fig. 3

Fig. 4

4. Cut an 1/8" wide strip of Gold Glitter long enough to wrap around the stone. Wrap the strip around the stone, pressing as you go to ensure the strip lays flat against the stone ***(Fig. 5)***. Trim and butt the ends together; smooth the seam with your fingertip.

Fig. 5

5. Glue a small rounded disk of Gold Glitter to the ring, making a base for the stone ***(Fig. 6)***; allow glue to dry.

Fig. 6

6. Taking care not to distort the clay, gently press the stone onto the base until it is firmly in place. Follow the manufacturer's instructions to bake and cool.

Lentil Bead Earrings continued

4. Place 1 ball under the lentil bead rolling tool. Keeping a consistent gentle pressure on the ball, rotate the tool in a circular motion. The ball will begin to take on a lentil shape and the colors will begin to swirl. Continue rotating until you are pleased with the look. The swirled bead should be approximately 1" in diameter. ***(Fig. 5)***. Repeat with the remaining ball.

Fig. 5

5. Use the needle tool to carefully make a hole through the center of each bead. Place on the bead baking cushion and follow the manufacturer's instructions to bake and cool.

6. Thread a lentil bead and a crystal bead on a head pin. Make a wrapped loop in the wire above the crystal bead. Slip the bead on an ear wire. Repeat to make the second earring.

Royal Statement Necklace

SHOPPING LIST

- ☐ premo! Sculpey Accents® Clay (2 oz): 2 pkgs of Gold
- ☐ premo! Sculpey® Clay (2 oz): 2 pkgs of Alizarin Crimson Hue
- ☐ Sculpey® Clay Conditioning Machine
- ☐ Sculpey® Super Slicer
- ☐ Sculpey® Bakeable Silicone Mold: Bezel Shapes
- ☐ Sculpey® Bakeable Silicone Mold: Cabochon Shapes
- ☐ premo! Sculpey® Circle Metal Cutters
- ☐ Sculpey® Style and Detail Tools
- ☐ Sculpey® Etch 'n Pearl
- ☐ Sculpey® Bake & Bond
- ☐ Sculpey® Acrylic Roller
- ☐ 20 gold eye pins
- ☐ 10" length of gold chain
- ☐ Gold toggle clasp
- ☐ 4 large gold jump rings
- ☐ Wire cutters and chain-nose pliers (2 pair)
- ☐ Super glue
- ☐ Spray bottle of water
- ☐ Damp paper towels or baby wipes

To make the Necklace:

Please read the General Instructions on pages 22- 23 before beginning your project.

Always lightly spray the molds with water before pressing clay into the molds.

1. Using the #1 setting on the clay machine, condition each color of clay from lightest to darkest.

2. To make the cabochons, roll a $3/4$" dia. ball of Alizarin Crimson. Firmly press the ball into the medium teardrop mold.

3. Working from the center toward the outer edges, use the Super Slicer to remove the excess clay from the mold ***(Fig. 1)***. Remove the teardrop from the mold ***(Fig. 2)***.

Fig. 1

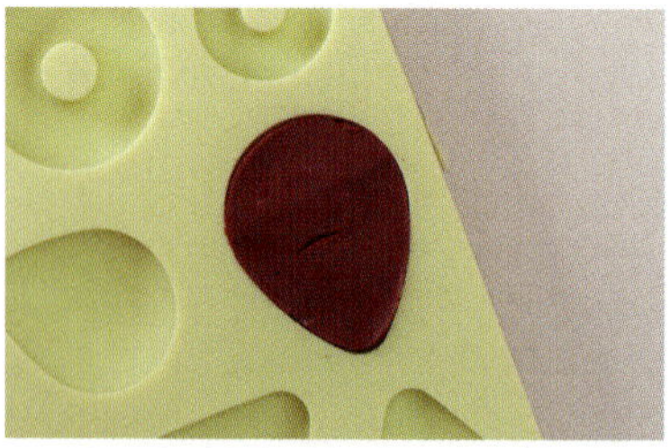

Fig. 2

4. Repeat Steps 2-3 to make 2 large teardrops, 2 small teardrops, 2 small triangles and 2 small rounds. Set the cabochons aside.

5. For the swirl cabochon, roll a $1/4$" x $2^1/2$" log of each clay color. Tightly twist the 2 logs together ***(Fig. 3)***. Roll the twisted log into a ball. Cut the ball in half and press the cut side into the large round mold ***(Fig. 4)***.

Fig. 3

Fig. 4

Designed by Syndee Holt

6. Trim and remove the cabochon as in Step 3. Rub the surface lightly with your fingertip to polish the micas in the clay.

7. For the bezels, run a small amount of Gold through the clay machine on the #1 setting. Fold the clay and run it through again on the #3 setting. Continue to fold and run the clay through the machine on the #3 setting until you have a smooth, even sheet of gold.

8. Identify the bezel mold sizes that fit your cabochons. Use the circle cutters to cut clay circles from the gold sheet that are slightly larger than the selected bezel molds ***(Fig. 5)***.

Fig. 5

9. Firmly press a clay circle into the matching bezel mold and fold the excess toward the center of the mold ***(Fig. 6)***. Trim and then remove the bezel as in Step 3 ***(Fig. 7)***. Repeat for each bezel needed.

Fig. 6

Fig. 7

10. Add a small drop of Bake and Bond to the center of a bezel and insert the matching cabochon. Use your fingers to gently press the bezel sides tight against the cabochon. Repeat for each bezel and cabochon.

11. Trim the eye pins to 3/8" long. For the medium teardrop bead, insert an eye pin into the top (narrow end) of the bead. For the marbled bead, insert one eye pin in the bottom of the bead and 2 eye pins (11:00 and 1:00) in the top of the bead. For the remaining beads, insert an eye pin in the top and bottom of each bead. **Note:** To allow the necklace to lay flat, insert all top eye pins perpendicular to the bead and all bottom eye pins horizontal with the bead ***(Fig. 8)***.

Fig. 8

12. To add the decoration to the bezel of the marbled bead, use the Etch 'n Pearl tool to make lines and dots around the bezel ***(Fig. 9-10)***.

Fig. 9

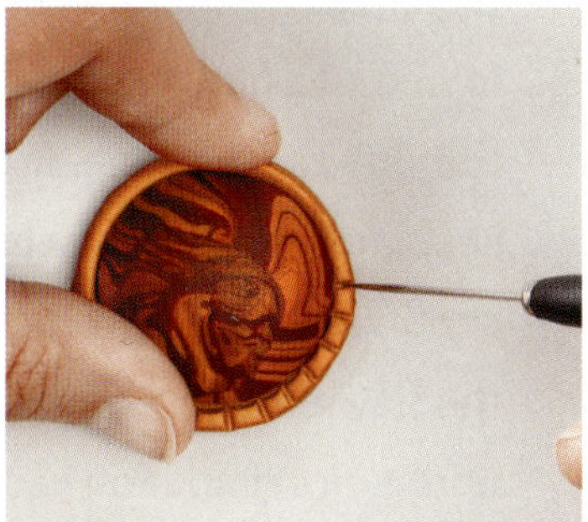

Fig. 10

13. Follow the manufacturer's instructions to bake and cool. Remove each eye pin and place a drop of super glue on the end of the pin; reinsert the pin and allow to dry.

14. Use the chain-nose pliers to open and close the eye pins (see below) to join the beads together. Cut the chain in half and attach one piece of the toggle clasp to each chain piece. Attach the remaining chain end to each side of the necklace.

Opening & Closing Jump Rings, Wire Loops & Eye Pins

Pick up a jump ring with chain-nose pliers. With a second pair of pliers, gently hold the other side of the ring. Open the ring by pulling one pair of pliers toward your while pushing the other pair away.

Close the ring by pushing and pulling the pliers in the opposite direction, bringing the ring ends back together. You will also open and close loops on eye pins in the same way.

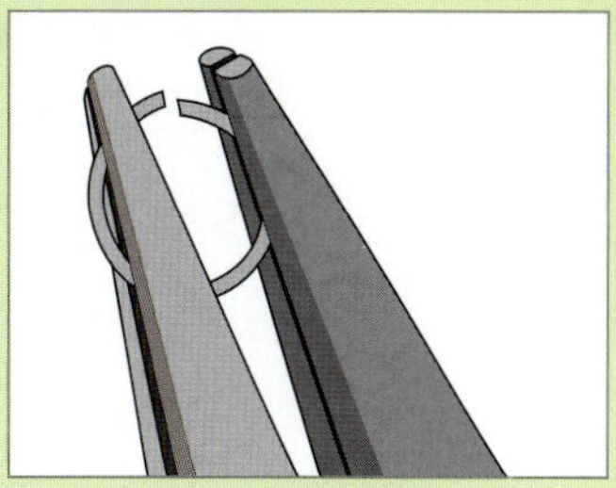

Flower Earrings

SHOPPING LIST

- ☐ Sculpey® III Clay (2 oz): 1 pkg ***each*** of Violet and Yellow
- ☐ Sculpey® Clay Conditioning Machine
- ☐ Sculpey® Clay Tool Starter Set
- ☐ Sculpey® Super Slicer
- ☐ Sculpey® Acrylic Roller
- ☐ $2^1/_4$" x $2^1/_4$" square cutter (we used a Wilton® Fondant Cutter)
- ☐ 2 6mm gold jump rings
- ☐ 2 4mm gold split rings
- ☐ 2 gold ear wires
- ☐ 2 4mm gold flat-backed crystals
- ☐ Chain-nose pliers (2 pair)
- ☐ Damp paper towels or baby wipes

To make the Earrings:

Please read the General Instructions on pages 22-23 before beginning your project.

1. Using the #2 setting on the clay machine, condition and roll out an approximately 3" x 3" x $^1/_8$" sheet of each color clay.

2. Use the cutter to cut a square from each color. Cut each square in half diagonally to make 2 triangles. Press one triangle of each color together to form a square ***(Fig. 1)***. Bringing the lower corners up to meet the top corners, fold the square in half ***(Fig. 2)***; press along fold to remove any air bubbles.

Fig. 1

Fig. 2

3. Using the #1 setting on the clay machine and inserting the folded side first, run the rectangle through the machine. Always keeping the same orientation continue folding and running the clay through the machine until a nice gradation in colors is achieved. Once satisfied with the gradation, run the clay through the machine on the #3 setting. Trim the clay to a rectangular shape ***(Fig. 3)***.

Fig. 3

Designed by Phoebe Doehring

4. Beginning with the yellow end, roll the rectangle into a tight log ***(Fig. 4)***. Continue rolling until the log is about 1/4" in diameter ***(Fig. 5)***.

Fig. 4

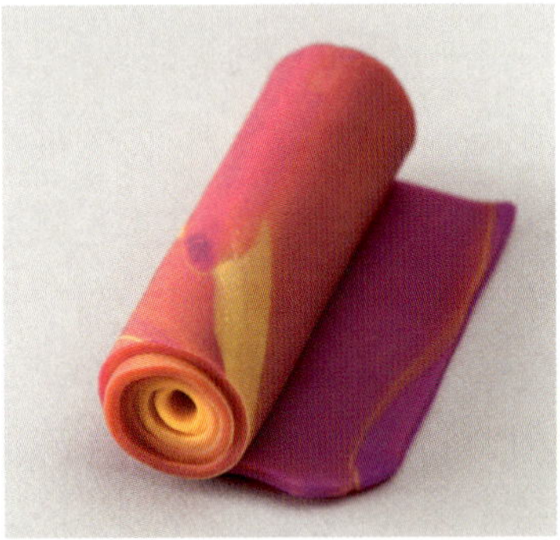

Fig. 5

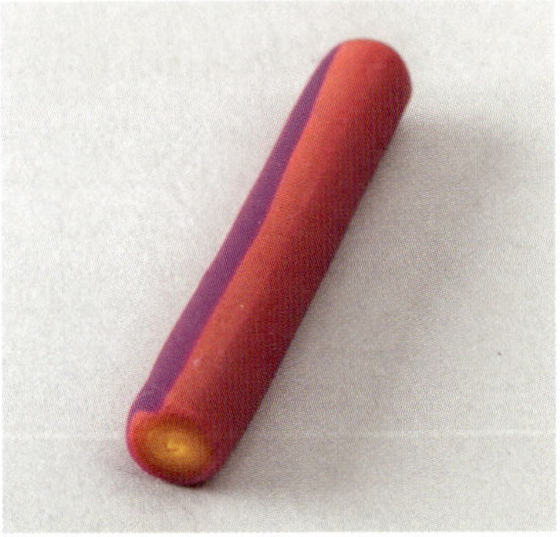

5. To make the petals, slice 10 pieces, each 1/8" thick from the log ***(Fig. 6)***. Shape each piece into a teardrop and flatten until the petals are about 1/2" long ***(Fig. 7)***.

Fig. 6

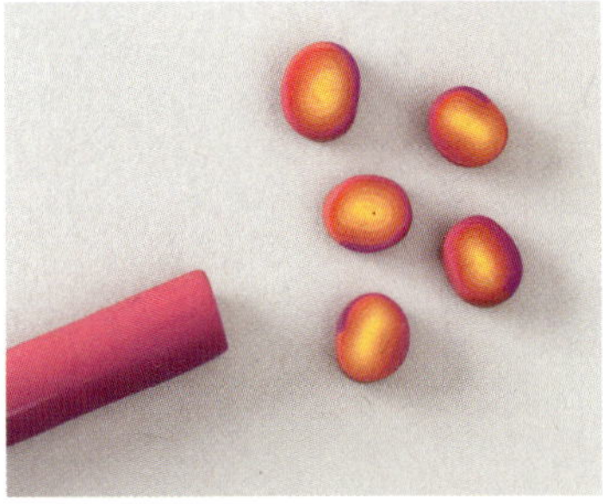

Fig. 7

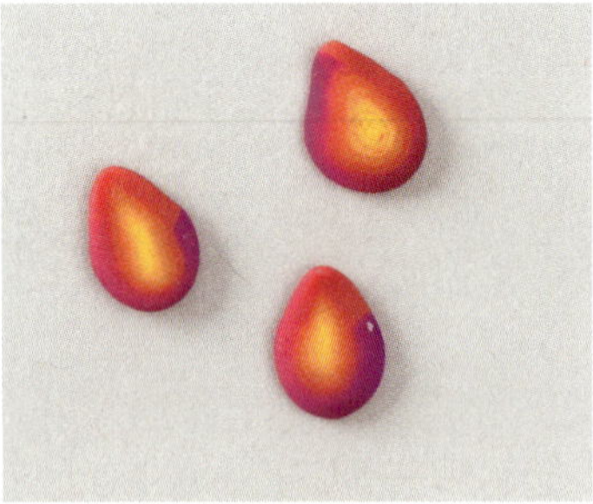

6. Make 4 vertical lines on each petal ***(Fig. 8)***. To scallop the edges, make small indentions on the wide end of each petal where the lines end ***(Fig. 9)***.

Fig. 8

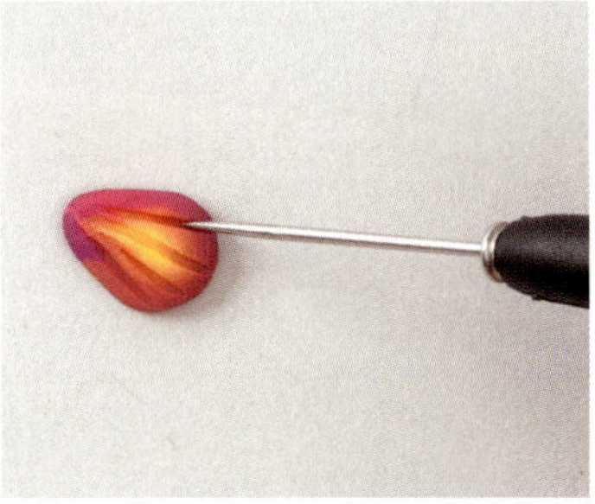

Fig. 9

7. Overlapping slightly ***(Fig. 10)***, arrange 5 petals into a flower shape; press gently to secure. Press a crystal in the center of the flower. Make a small hole in the top of one petal. Repeat using the remaining petals and crystal to make the second flower. Follow the manufacturer's instructions to bake and cool.

Fig. 10

8. Use the pliers to attach a jump ring (page 11) to each flower. Slide each jump ring onto a split ring; slide the split ring onto an ear wires.

Antique Necklace

Shown on page 17.

SHOPPING LIST

- ☐ Sculpey® Soufflé Clay (1.7 oz): 1 pkg ***each*** of Bluestone and Igloo
- ☐ Sculpey® Clay Conditioning Machine
- ☐ Sculpey® Acrylic Clay Roller
- ☐ Sculpey® Clay Tool Starter Set
- ☐ Sculpey® Flexible Texture Sheets - Landscape
- ☐ premo! Sculpey® Circle Metal Cutters
- ☐ premo! Sculpey® Tear Drop Metal Cutters
- ☐ Translucent Liquid Sculpey®
- ☐ Non-scratch scouring pad
- ☐ White acrylic paint and a small paintbrush
- ☐ Damp paper towels or baby wipes
- ☐ 40" of 1/4"-1/2" wide ribbon
- ☐ Spray bottle with water

To make the Necklace:

Please read the General Instructions on pages 22- 23 before beginning your project.

1. Using the #2 setting on the clay machine, condition and roll out a 1 1/2" x 1 1/2" sheet of Igloo.

2. For texture, lightly press the scouring pad into the clay sheet. Cut a 1" tear drop from the sheet ***(Fig. 1)***. Place the 3/4" tear drop cutter on the clay tear drop, centered side to side but leaving a slightly thicker edge around the bottom of the tear drop; cut out ***(Fig. 2)***. Follow the manufacturer's instructions to bake and cool.

Fig. 1

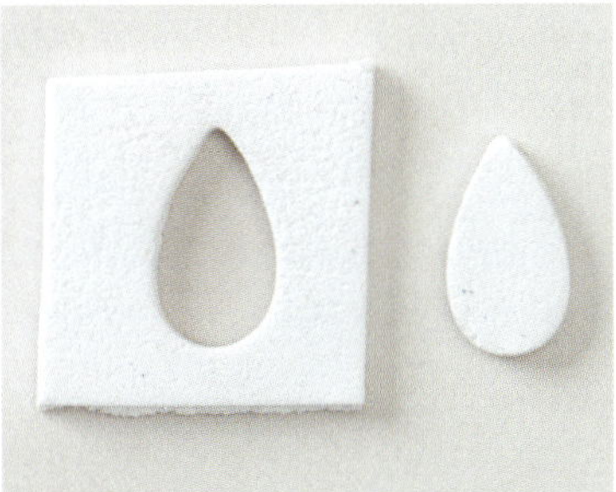

Fig. 2

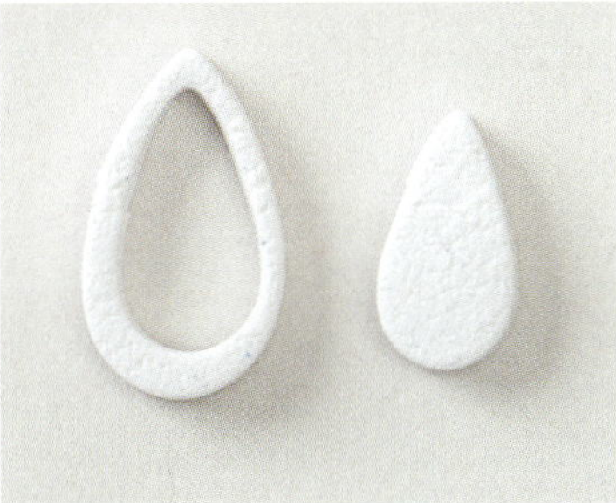

3. Using the #1 setting on the clay machine, condition and roll out a 2 1/2" x 2 1/2" sheet of Bluestone. Spray a light mist of water over the surface of the clay. Center the Dandelion Texture Sheet on the clay and use the acrylic roller to press the sheet into the clay square. Remove the sheet and pat dry. For texture, lightly press the scouring pad into the clay sheet ***(Fig. 3)***.

Fig. 3

4. Centering the dandelion design, use the Circle Cutter to cut a 2" circle from the square. With the point facing the circle center, position about 2/3's of the 1" teardrop cutter on the circle; make the cut and remove the teardrop wedge ***(Fig. 4)***.

Fig. 4

5. Apply Translucent Liquid Sculpey to the point and 2/3's of the way up outer sides of the teardrop ring. Press the teardrop ring into the open wedge of the circle ***(Fig. 5)***. Use the Needle Tool to remove any excess clay that may squeeze into the ring opening. Follow the manufacturer's instructions to bake and cool.

Fig. 5

6. Apply a coat of paint to the entire surface of the medallion, making sure the paints goes down into the indentions. Use a damp paper towel or baby wipe to remove the excess paint from the surface ***(Fig. 6)***. Follow the manufacturer's instructions to bake and cool.

Fig. 6

7. Fold the ribbon in half and tie the ends together with an overhand knot. Attach the folded end of the ribbon to the teardrop with a Larks Head Knot ***(Fig. 7)***.

Fig. 7

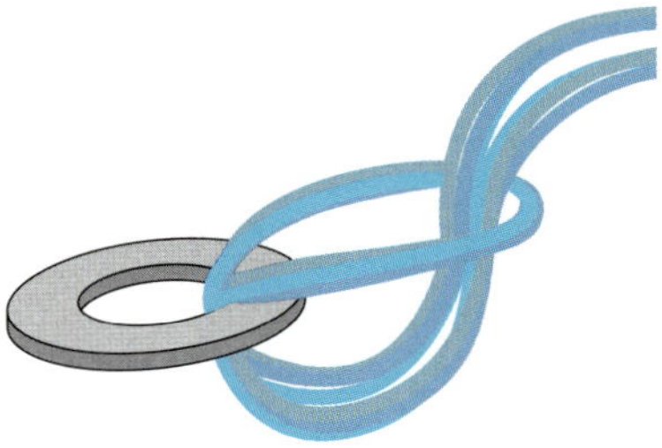

Designed by Gretchen Amberg

Lots of Dots Bracelet

SHOPPING LIST

- ☐ Sculpey® Soufflé Clay (1.7 oz): 1 pkg ***each*** of Canary, Pumpkin, Cherry Pie, So 80's, Turnip, Robin's Egg, Lagoon, Jade, Pistachio, and Igloo
- ☐ Sculpey® Clay Conditioning Machine
- ☐ Sculpey® Bead Making Kit
- ☐ Sculpey® Bead Maker
- ☐ Sculpey® Acrylic Roller
- ☐ Silver jewelry wire
- ☐ 10 silver spacer beads
- ☐ Silver crimp beads
- ☐ Silver lobster clasp
- ☐ Crimp tool, wire cutters
- ☐ Damp paper towels or baby wipes

To make the Bracelet:

Please read the General Instructions on pages 22- 23 before beginning your project.

Our bracelet is about 8 1/2" long. To adjust the length, add or delete beads as needed.

1. Using the #2 setting on the clay machine and working with one color at a time from lightest to darkest, condition each color of clay.

2. Refer to the Bead Maker package instructions to roll one 16mm ball of each color except Igloo ***(Fig. 1)***. Use the needle tool to make a hole through the center of each bead.

Fig. 1

Designed by Phoebe Doehring

3. For the dots on **each** bead, you will need 12 small dots of Igloo, 12 medium dots of one color and 12 tiny dots of a coordinating color (see chart, page 21, for color combinations).

4. To make each bead, roll a 2" x 1/8" dia. log of the medium dot color, a 2" x 1/32" dia. log of the tiny dot color, and a 2" x 1/16" dia. log of Igloo ***(Fig. 2)***. Cut 12 equal size slices from each log and roll into dots ***(Fig. 3)***.

Fig. 2

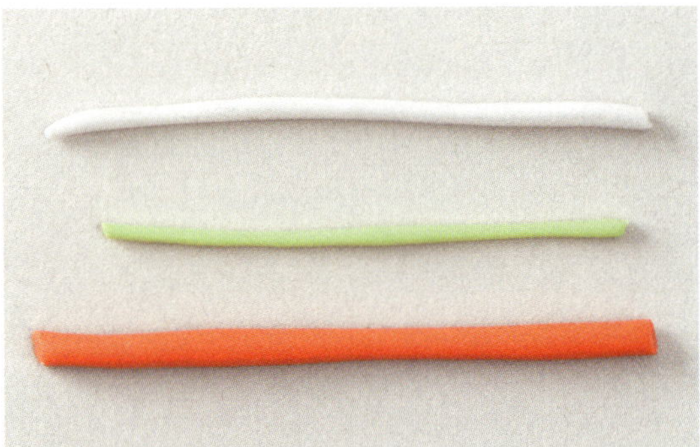

Fig. 3

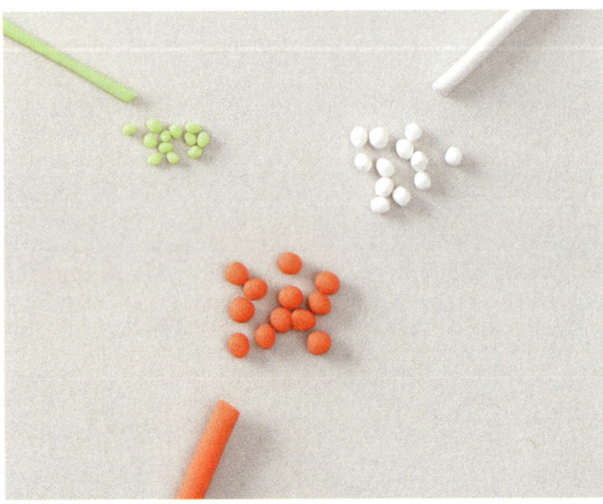

5. Keeping the spacing even, press the medium dots onto the bead ***(Fig. 4)***. Press the coordinating tiny dots into the centers of the medium dots. Press the 12 small Igloo dots into the spaces between the other dots.

Fig. 4

6. Follow the manufacturer's instructions to use the Bead Baking Rack; cool beads completely.

7. Cut a 10" length of jewelry wire. Thread one end of the wire through a crimp bead, one piece of the lobster clasp, and back through the crimp bead ***(Fig 5)***. Leaving about 1/2" tail, crimp the bead (see **Using Crimp Beads**) with the crimp tool. Beginning and ending with a spacer bead, alternately thread beads and spacer beads on the wire. Thread the wire end through a crimp bead wire, the remaining clasp piece and back through the crimp bead. Pull the wire end to tighten. Crimp the bead and trim the wire end.

Fig. 5

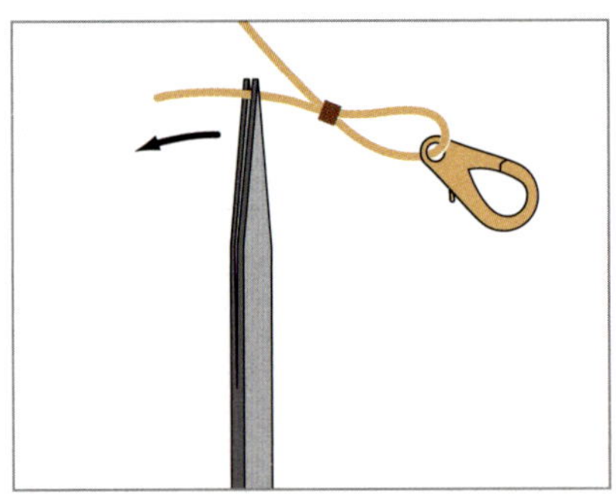

Using Crimp Beads

1. Place the crimp bead on the inner groove of the crimp tool and squeeze *(Fig. 1)*.
2. Release the tool, turn the crimp bead a quarter turn and place it in the outer groove *(Fig. 2)*.
3. Squeeze the tool to round the crimp bead *(Fig. 3)*.

Fig. 1

Fig. 2

Fig. 3

Bead Color Chart

Bead Color	Small Dots	Medium Dots	Tiny Dots
Canary	Igloo	Pumpkin	Pistachio
Pumpkin	Igloo	Cherry Pie	Canary
Cherry Pie	Igloo	So 80's	Pumpkin
So 80's	Igloo	Turnip	Cherry Pie
Turnip	Igloo	Robin's Egg	So 80's
Robin's Egg	Igloo	Lagoon	Turnip
Lagoon	Igloo	Jade	Robin's Egg
Jade	Igloo	Pistachio	Lagoon
Pistachio	Igloo	Canary	Jade

GENERAL INSTRUCTIONS

Basic Tools and Supplies

It is best to use clay dedicated tools. The tools and supplies listed below are used in almost all the projects. Your project instructions may include other tools specific to that project.

- Sculpey® Clay Conditioning Machine - used to condition clay to make it more pliable and to roll sheets of clay to the desired thickness.
- Sculpey® Acrylic Roller - this non-stick roller is used to smooth and roll sheets of clay. Also used to press landscape sheets into the surface of the clay or press layers of clay together.
- Sculpey® Clay Tool Starter Set is a versatile set that contains 3 double-ended tools that are used to create lines, holes, indentions, details, and cut clay.
- Sculpey® Super Slicer Set - this tool includes 4 interchangeable blades that allow you to cut clay easily.
- Sculpey® Work n' Bake Clay Mat, wax paper, aluminum foil, or a metal baking sheet to protect the work surface
- Sculpey® Work n' Bake Clay Mat, glass baking dish, metal pan or cookie sheet covered with parchment paper or aluminum foil, ceramic tile, for baking

Conditioning Clay

Never place unbaked clay on unprotected furniture, countertops, or food prep surfaces. Always wash hands after handling clay and between colors.

- Begin with clean hands and a clean work surface. Cover your work surface with wax paper or aluminum foil or use a metal cookie sheet.
- Using the amount of clay called for in your project instructions, soften the clay by kneading it with your hands. To knead, roll the clay into a ball, then flatten the ball slightly and fold it over on itself; re-roll into a ball and repeat until the clay is soft and pliable.
- You can also condition your clay by running it through a Sculpey® Clay Conditioning Machine. Refer to the manufacturer's instructions for set up and use. If conditioning a block or large amount of clay, first flatten with the acrylic roller until the clay is only slightly thicker than opening between the rollers.
- If the clay ever becomes too warm, soft, and sticky, place it in a cool area until it firms up and loses the stickiness.

Rolling Clay Sheets

Clay sheets can be rolled by hand or using your clay conditioning machine.

- To roll sheets by hand, slightly flatten a conditioned clay ball between your palms to make a pancake.
- Place 2 dowels (the diameter of your desired clay sheet thickness) on either side of the pancake. ***Note:*** Using dowels, strips of cardstock, or thin strips of cardboard as guides when rolling sheets will keep the thickness of the clay consistent.
- With the roller riding on the dowels, roll over the clay until it is completely flattened.
- To roll sheets using your Sculpey® Clay Conditioning Machine, refer to the manufacturer's instructions.

Baking Clay

Do not use a microwave oven. Never exceed the recommended oven temperature or baking time. Bake in a well-ventilated area.

- Preheat oven to 275ºF (135º C). For best results, check temperature with an oven thermometer.
- Use a glass baking dish, a metal pan or a cookie sheet, or a Sculpey® Work n' Bake Clay Mat when baking clay. If you are using a clay dedicated baking dish or pan, you can place the clay directly on the surface. Any dishes or pans that may be used later for food should be covered with parchment paper or aluminum foil.
- Baking times vary depending on the type of clay. Follow manufacturer's instructions for baking time. Baking should be completed by an adult.

Safety Tips

- Do not bake clay in a microwave oven.
- Never exceed the recommended oven temperature or baking time.
- Bake in a well-ventilated area.
- Do not ingest clay.
- Do not use clay items for food.
- POLYMER CLAY MAY STAIN OR DAMAGE UNPROTECTED FURNITURE OR FINISHED SURFACES. DO NOT USE polymer clay on unprotected surfaces. We recommend working on a Sculpey® Work n' Bake Clay Mat, wax paper, metal baking sheet, or aluminum foil.

Production Team: Technical Writer – Jean Lewis; Technical Associate – Mary Sullivan Hutcheson; Editorial Writer – Susan Frantz Wiles; Senior Graphic Artist – Lora Puls; Graphic Artist – Sharvil Salve; Photostylist – Sondra Daniel; and Photographer – Ken West.